python

Python Programming

Skill Level : Basic

Python Programming

 python

Plan:

python guideline

Regles

Examples

Exercises

Solutions

Conclusion

 python

python guideline

Starting to code in Python is a great choice! Python is known for its simplicity and readability, making it an excellent language for beginners. Here's a step-by-step guideline to help you get started:

 python

python guideline

1. Install Python:

- Visit the <u>official Python website</u>.
- Go to the "Downloads" section and download the latest version of Python for your operating system (Windows, macOS, or Linux).
- Follow the installation instructions provided on the website.

 python

python guideline

2. Choose a Text Editor or IDE:

- Python code can be written in a simple text editor or a more feature-rich Integrated Development Environment (IDE).
- For beginners, popular choices include:
  - Text Editors: Visual Studio Code, Sublime Text, Atom.
  - IDEs: PyCharm, Thonny, Jupyter Notebook (great for data science).

 python

Certainly! Python is a versatile and widely-used programming language known for its simplicity and readability. Here's a brief overview of text-based coding in Python, along with some fundamental concepts in computer science and programming:

 python

1. Basic Python Syntax:

Variables:

In Python, variables are used to store and manage data. They act as placeholders for values, making it easier to work with and manipulate data in a program. Here's a brief explanation of variables in Python:

python

1. Operators (+, −, *, /, //, %, **):

A. Addition (+):

Adds two numbers.

Example:

```
result = 5 + 3
print(result)
```

Result

8

python

1. Operators (+, –, *, /, //, %, **):

B. Subtraction (-):

Subtracts the right operand from the left operand.

Example:

```python
result = 5 - 3
print(result)
```

Result

2

python

1. Operators (+, -, *, /, //, %, **):

B. Multiplication (*):

Multiplies two numbers.

Example:

```python
result = 5 * 3
print(result)
```

Result

15

python

1. Operators (+, -, *, /, //, %, **):

B. Division (/):

Divides the left operand by the right operand (returns a float).

Example:

```
result = 15 / 3
print(result)
```

Result

5.0

python

1. Operators (+, −, *, /, //, %, **):

B. Floor Division (//):

Divides the left operand by the right operand and returns the integer part of the result.

Example:

```python
result = 17 // 5
print(result)
```

Result

3

python

1. Operators (+, −, *, /, //, %, **):

B. Modulus (%):

Returns the remainder when the left operand is divided by the right operand.

Example:

```python
result = 17 % 5
print(result)
```

Result

2

python

1. Operators (+, −, *, /, //, %, **):

B. Exponentiation (*):

Raises the left operand to the power of the right operand.

Example:

```python
result = 2 ** 3
print(result)
```

Result

8

 python

2. Variable Assignment :

Example:

```
x = 5
name = "John"
```

Explanation :

In the above examples, x is assigned the value 5, and name is assigned the string "John". Python is dynamically typed, meaning you don't need to explicitly declare the type of a variable; Python infers it based on the assigned value.

 python

3. Naming Conventions :

Rule : ⚠️

➡️ Variable names can include letters, numbers, and underscores.

➡️ They cannot start with a number.

➡️ Variable names are case-sensitive (age and Age would be different variables).

 python

4. Data Types :

➡️ Variables in Python can hold
    different types of data:

Example:

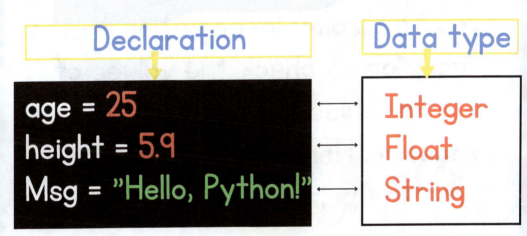

Declaration	Data type
age = 25	⟷ Integer
height = 5.9	⟷ Float
Msg = "Hello, Python!"	⟷ String

 python

5. Print Statement:

In Python, the print() statement is used to output text or data to the console. It is a fundamental way to display information to the user or to check the values of variables during program execution. Here's an explanation of the print() statement:

 python

Example: Print Statement in Python

```
print("Welcome to Python!")
```

Result

Welcome to Python!

6. Input

Description:

In Python, you can take user input using the input() function.

 python

Example:

```
name = input("Enter your name: ")
print("Hello, " + name + " to  Python")
```

Result
↓

Enter your name:
Your name

Hello, your name to Python

In this example, the input("Enter your name: ") statement prompts the user to enter their name. The entered value is then stored in the variable name, and the program prints a greeting using that input.

 python

6. Input

Exercise:

Write a program that takes the user's age and favorite color as input and prints a message with this information.

 python

6. Input

Solution:

```python
age = input("Enter your age: ")
color = input("Enter your favorite color: ")
print("You are " + age + " years old and your
favorite color is " + color + ".")
```

This exercise demonstrates how to use the input() function to capture multiple pieces of information from the user and incorporate them into a printed message.

 python

7. Indentation:

Python uses indentation (whitespace) to define blocks of code. It's crucial to be consistent with indentation, and four spaces per level is a common convention.

 python

7. Indentation:

Example:

```python
if x > 5:
print("x is greater than 5")
```

 python

8. Naming Conventions:

- Use descriptive variable and function names.
- Variable names are typically lowercase with words separated by underscores (snake_case).
- Function names follow the same convention.

python

8. Naming Conventions:

Example:

```python
my_variable = 42
def calculate_sum(a, b):
return a + b
```

python

9. Comments:

- Use comments to explain complex parts of your code.
- Follow the PEP 8 style guide for comments.

 python

9. Comments :

Example:

```
# This is a single-line comment


"""
This is a multi-line comment. It
can span multiple lines.

"""
```

 python

10. Docstrings :

Include docstrings to provide documentation for functions, classes, and modules.

 python

II. Docstrings :

Example:

```python
def my_function(param):
    """
    This is a docstring that explains
    what my_function does.
    Parameters: - param: An input
    parameter. Returns: - The result
    of the function.
    """
    return param * 2
```

 python

12. Imports :

- Import modules at the top of your script or module.
- Follow the PEP 8 style guide for imports.

 python

12. Imports :

Example:

```python
import math
from module import function
```

 python

13. Whitespace :

- Use a single space around binary operators.
- Avoid extraneous whitespace at the end of lines.

 python

13. Whitespace :

Example:

```
result = x + y
```

 python

14. Avoid Global Variables:

- Minimize the use of global variables.
- Use function parameters and return values instead.

 python

14. Avoid Global Variables:

Example:

```python
def calculate_total(price, quantity):
    return price * quantity
```

 python

15. Exception Handling:

- Use try, except blocks for exception handling.
- Be specific about the exceptions you catch.

 python

15. Exception Handling:

Example:

```python
try:
result = x / y
except ZeroDivisionError:
print("Cannot divide by zero.")
```

 python

16. List and Dictionary Comprehensions

- Use list comprehensions for concise and readable code when creating lists.

- Similar comprehensions can be applied to dictionaries.

 python

16. List and Dictionary Comprehensions

Example:

```python
squares = [x**2 for x in range(10)]
```

 python

17. Avoid Magic Numbers:

- Avoid using "magic numbers" (hard-coded numerical values without explanation). Use named constants or variables instead.

 python

17. Avoid Magic Numbers:

Example:

```python
MAX_RETRIES = 3
for _ in range(MAX_RETRIES):
# code here
```

 python

Conditional Statements:

Description:

Control flow in Python refers to the order in which the interpreter executes statements in a script. It involves making decisions (conditional statements) and repeating actions (loops). Here are some key aspects of control flow in Python:

 python

If Statement

Example:

```
x = 10
if x > 5:

print("x is greater than 5")
```

Result

x is greater than 5

 python

Conditional Statements:

Exercise 1 :

Write a program that takes the user's age as input and prints "You are an adult" if the age is 18 or older, otherwise print "You are a minor."

 python

Conditional Statements:

Solution:

```python
age = int(input("Enter your age: "))
if age >= 18:
print("You are an adult.")
else:
print("You are a minor.")
```

python

If-else Statement:

Example:

```python
y = 3
if y > 5:
print("y is greater than 5")
else :
print("y is not greater than 5")
```

Result

⬇

y is not greater than 5

 python

Conditional Statements:

Exercise 1 :

Write a program that takes a number as input and prints "Positive" if the number is greater than 0, "Negative" if it's less than 0, and "Zero" if it's equal to 0.

 python

Conditional Statements:

Solution:

```python
number = float(input("Enter a number: "))
if number > 0:
print("Positive")
elif number < 0:
print("Negative")
else:
print("Zero")
```

 python

If-elif-else Statement:

Example:

```python
z = 7
if z > 10:
  print("z is greater than 10")
elif z > 5:
 print("z is greater than 5 but not 10")
else:
 print("z is 5 or less")
```

Result

z is greater than 5 but not 10

 python

Conditional Statements:

Exercise 1 :

Write a program that takes a person's height in meters and weight in kilograms, then calculates their BMI (Body Mass Index) and prints "Underweight," "Normal," "Overweight," or "Obese" based on the BMI.

 python

Conditional Statements:

Solution:

```python
height = float(input("Enter your
height in meters: "))
weight = float(input("Enter your
weight in kilograms: "))
bmi = weight / (height ** 2)
if bmi < 18.5:
print("Underweight")
elif 18.5 <= bmi < 25:
print("Normal")
elif 25 <= bmi < 30:
print("Overweight")
else:
 print("Obese")
```

 python

A - For Loop:

Description:

Certainly! The for loop in Python is used to iterate over a sequence (such as a list, tuple, string, dictionary, or range) and execute a block of code for each item in the sequence. The general syntax of a for loop is as follows:

 python

A – For Loop:

```
for variable in sequence:
    # Code to be executed for each item in the sequence
```

Here's a breakdown of the components:

- for keyword: Initiates the loop.
- variable: Represents the variable that will take on each value in the sequence during each iteration.
- in keyword: Specifies the sequence to iterate over.
- sequence: The iterable object (e.g., list, tuple, string, range) that provides the values for the variable.

 python

For Loop

Example: 1

```python
fruits = ["apple", "banana", "cherry"]
for fruit in fruits:
print(fruit)
```

Result

apple
banana
cherry

 python

A – For Loop:

Explication :

IN THIS EXAMPLE:
- The for loop iterates over the fruits list.
- In each iteration, the variable fruit takes on the value of the current item in the list.

The indented block of code (the print statement) is executed for each item, printing each fruit on a new line.

 python

A - For Loop:

Range Function with For Loop:

The range() function is often used for loops to generate a sequence of numbers. The range() function generates a sequence of numbers up to, but not including, a specified number.

For Loop

Example 2 :

```python
word = "Python"
for letter in word:
print(letter)
```

Result

P
y
t
h
o
n

 python

For Loop

Exercise 1 :

Write a program that calculates the sum of all numbers from 1 to 100 using a for loop.

 python

For Loop

Solution 1 :

```python
sum_numbers = 0
for num in range(1, 101):
sum_numbers += num
print("Sum of numbers
from 1 to 100:",
sum_numbers)
```

Result

Sum of numbers from 1 to 100:
5050

 python

B – While Loop:

Description:

The while loop in Python is used to repeatedly execute a block of code as long as a specified condition is true. The general syntax of a while loop is as follows:

 python

B – While Loop:

syntax :

```
while condition:
# Code to be executed as long as the condition is true
```

Here's an explanation of the components:

- while keyword: Initiates the loop.
- condition: Specifies the condition that must be true for the loop to continue executing.
- Code inside the while loop: The indented block of code that will be executed repeatedly as long as the condition is true.

While Loop:

Example: 1

```python
count = 1
while count <= 5:
print(count) count += 1
```

Result

1
2
3
4
5

 python

While Loop:

Explication :

IN THIS EXAMPLE:
- The while loop continues as long as the condition count <= 5 is true.
- In each iteration, the indented block of code is executed, which includes printing the current value of count and incrementing it by 1.

 python

While Loop:

Using break and continue in a While Loop:

- The break statement is used to exit the loop prematurely based on a certain condition.
- The continue statement is used to skip the rest of the code inside the loop for the current iteration and move to the next iteration.

While Loop:
break and continue in While Loop: Example :

```python
num = 1
while num <= 10:
if num == 5:
break
elif num % 2 == 0:
num += 1
continue
print(num) num += 1
```

Result

1
3

 python

While Loop:

Explication :

IN THIS EXAMPLE:

- The loop exits when num is equal to 5 due to the break statement.
- The continue statement skips the even numbers, and the odd numbers are printed.

 python

Exercise 1 :

SIMPLE CALCULATOR

Write a Python program that takes two numbers as input and prints their sum.

 **python**

Solution Execcise 1:

SIMPLE CALCULATOR

```python
num1 = float(input("Enter the first number: "))
num2 = float(input("Enter the second number: "))
result = num1 + num2
print("Sum:", result)
```

Result

Enter the first number: 3
Enter the second number: 4.5
Sum: 7.5

 python

Exercices

Explanation Exercise 1 :

SIMPLE CALCULATOR

- The input() function is used to get user input.
- The input is converted to floating-point numbers using float().
- The sum is calculated and printed.

 python

Exercise 2 :

TEMPERATURE CONVERTER

Write a Python program that
converts Celsius to Fahrenheit.

 python

Solution Execcise 2:

TEMPERATURE CONVERTER

```python
celsius = float(input("Enter temperature in
Celsius: "))
fahrenheit = (celsius * 9/5) + 32
print("Temperature in Fahrenheit:",
fahrenheit)
```

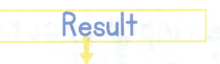 Result

Enter temperature in Celsius: 25
Temperature in Fahrenheit: 77.0

 python

Exercices

Explanation Exercise 2 :

TEMPERATURE CONVERTER

- The formula (Celsius * 9/5) + 32 is used for temperature conversion.
- User input is converted to a floating-point number.
- The converted temperature is printed.

 python

Exercices

Exercise 3

SUM OF EVEN NUMBERS

Write a Python program to calculate the sum of numbers from 1 to 10.

 python

Solution Execcise 3:

SUM OF EVEN NUMBERS

```python
sum_numbers = 0
for num in range(1, 11):
sum_numbers += num
print("Sum of numbers:", sum_numbers)
```

 Result

Sum of numbers: 55

 python

Exercices

Explanation Exercise 3 :

SUM OF EVEN NUMBERS

- We use a for loop to iterate through numbers from 1 to 10.
- In each iteration, the current number is added to the sum_numbers variable.
- Finally, the sum is printed.

 python

 Exercices

Exercise 4 :

MULTIPLICATION TABLE

Write a Python program to print the multiplication table for the number 5.

 python

Solution Execcise 4:

MULTIPLICATION TABLE

```python
number = 5
for i in range(1, 11):
result = number * i
 print(f"{number} x {i} = {result}")
```

Result

```
5 x 1 = 5
5 x 2 = 10
5 x 3 = 15
5 x 4 = 20
5 x 5 = 25
5 x 6 = 30
5 x 7 = 35
5 x 8 = 40
5 x 9 = 45
5 x 10 = 50
```

 python

Exercices

Explanation Exercise 4 :

MULTIPLICATION TABLE

- We use a for loop to iterate through numbers from 1 to 10.
- In each iteration, the product of 5 and the current number is calculated and printed.

 python

Exercices

Exercise 5 :

MULTIPLICATION TABLE

Write a Python program to print the multiplication table for the number 5.

python

Solution Execcise 5:

MULTIPLICATION TABLE

```python
number = 5
for i in range(1, 11):
result = number * i
 print(f"{number} x {i} = {result}")
```

Result

```
5 x 1 = 5
5 x 2 = 10
5 x 3 = 15
5 x 4 = 20
5 x 5 = 25
5 x 6 = 30
5 x 7 = 35
5 x 8 = 40
5 x 9 = 45
5 x 10 = 50
```

 python

Exercices

MULTIPLICATION TABLE

- We use a for loop to iterate through numbers from 1 to 10.
- In each iteration, the product of 5 and the current number is calculated and printed.

 python

Exercices

Exercise 6 :

STRING CONCATENATION

Write a Python program that takes your name and age as input and prints a message using string concatenation.

 python

Solution Execcise 6:

STRING CONCATENATION

```python
name = input("Enter your name: ")
age = int(input("Enter your age: "))
message = "Hello, " + name + "! You are "
+ str(age) + " years old."
print(message)
```

Result

Enter your name: AliceEnter your age: 25
Hello, Alice! You are 25 years old.

 python

Exercices

Explanation Exercise 6 :

STRING CONCATENATION

- The input() function is used to get the user's name and age.
- String concatenation (+) is used to create the message.
- The str() function is used to convert the age (an integer) to a string for concatenation.

 python

 Exercices

Exercise 7 :

ODD OR EVEN

Write a Python program that takes a number as input and prints whether it's odd or even.

 python

Solution Execcise 7:

ODD OR EVEN

```python
number = int(input("Enter a number: "))
if number % 2 == 0:
print(number, "is even.")
else:
print(number, "is odd.")
```

Result

Enter a number: 7
7 is odd.

 python

Exercices

Explanation Exercise 7 :

ODD OR EVEN

- The input() function is used to get a number from the user.
- The if statement checks if the number is even (number % 2 == 0) and prints the result accordingly.

 python

 Exercices

Exercise 8 :

AREA OF A RECTANGLE

Write a Python program that takes the length and width of a rectangle as input and calculates its area.

 python

Solution Execcise 8:

AREA OF A RECTANGLE

```python
length = float(input("Enter the length of the rectangle: "))
width = float(input("Enter the width of the rectangle: "))
area = length * width
print("Area of the rectangle:", area)
```

 Result

Enter the length of the rectangle: 5
Enter the width of the rectangle: 8
Area of the rectangle: 40.0

 python

Exercices

Explanation Exercise 8 :

AREA OF A RECTANGLE

- The input() function is used to get the length and width as floating-point numbers.

- The area is calculated using the formula length * width.

 python

Conclusion

Here's a brief summary and some concluding thoughts for your Python lessons:

 python

Conclusion

Key Concepts Covered:

1. Variables and Data Types:
   - Understanding different data types such as integers, floats, strings, and booleans.
   - Declaring variables and assigning values.

 python

Conclusion suit

Key Concepts Covered:

1. Operators:
   - Arithmetic operators (+, -, *, /, //, %, **).
   - Comparison operators (==, !=, <, >, <=, >=).
   - Logical operators (and, or, not).
2. Control Flow:
   - Conditional statements (if, elif, else) for decision-making.
   - Loop structures (for, while) for repetitive tasks.

 python

Conclusion suit

Key Concepts Covered:

1. User Input:
   - Using the input() function to get user input.
   - Converting input to appropriate data types.
2. Functions:
   - Defining and using functions to encapsulate and reuse code.
   - Returning values from functions.

python

Conclusion suit

Key Concepts Covered:

1. User Input:
   - Using the input() function to get user input.
   - Converting input to appropriate data types.
2. Functions:
   - Defining and using functions to encapsulate and reuse code.
   - Returning values from functions.

 python

Conclusion suit

Practical Applications:

1. Simple Calculations: Performing basic arithmetic calculations and solving mathematical problems.
2. Decision-Making: Writing programs that make decisions based on conditions.
3. Repetitive Tasks: Automating repetitive tasks using loops.
4. User Interaction: Building programs that interact with the user through input and output.
5. Problem-Solving: Applying programming concepts to solve real-world problems.